THE BOOK OF
HAYLING ISLAND
and Langstone

MORE THAN A MILLENNIUM

THE BOOK OF
HAYLING ISLAND
and Langstone

MORE THAN A MILLENNIUM

Peter Rogers

HALSGROVE

First published in 2000 by Halsgrove
Copyright © 2000 Peter N. Rogers

ISBN 1 84114 078 3

British Library Cataloguing-in-Publication-Data
A CIP data for this book is available from the British Library

HALSGROVE
Halsgrove House
Lower Moor Way
Tiverton EX16 6SS
T: 01884 243242
F: 01884 243325
www.halsgrove.com

Printed and bound in Great Britain
by MPG Ltd, Bodmin

Contents

Preface		*9*
Introduction		*11*
Chapter 1	**The Archaeology of Hayling Island**	17
Chapter 2	**Langstone, Village and Harbour**	21
Chapter 3	**The Island Scene**	46
Chapter 4	**Hayling Island – A Postcard Miscellany**	81
Chapter 5	**The Pycroft Family**	99
Chapter 6	**Alexander McKee O.B.E. – Sub-aqua Explorer**	103
Chapter 7	**Hayling Island in the Second World War**	109
Chapter 8	**Ferry Point and The Norfolk Inn**	127
Chapter 9	**John Marshall and Seacourt**	129
Subscribers		*141*

For Audrey

Preface

It has long been felt that a volume devoted entirely to the pictorial history of both Hayling Island and Langstone (village and harbour) would be a welcome addition to the historical and photographic records of the Borough of Havant. The author will not be embarking upon a comprehensive history of Hayling or Langstone, as these tasks having been competently and successfully accomplished in the past by Charles John Longcroft with his *Hundred of Bosmere*, F.G.S.Thomas with *The King Holds Hayling* and various works on Langstone by John Morley, Richard Joicey and Havant Borough Council.

Numerous other (often privately published) treatises have appeared over many years, but they have most often been little more than fragmented versions of the long and interesting history of the two communities.

Hayling's lost and unique railway system, has been adequately dealt with in the several worthy volumes compiled by devoted enthusiasts; it is not intended therefore, to make more than a passing reference to the several pictures depicting the 'Hayling Billy' line. Neither will the author comment on, endorse or give credence to, tales of smugglers, ghosts or secret tunnels!

The Author's last contribution to the Hayling / Langstone story was in 1985 when European Libraries of the Netherlands published *The Borough of Havant in Old Picture Postcards*. That volume (now out of print) contained 43 photographs of Hayling Island and Langstone; it is intended that the scope of this present publication will extend to over 200 pictorial images of Hayling with Langstone. Readers familiar with the original book of postcards will possibly recognise in the current work, several views taken from that earlier publication; the reason being that, because of their rarity value and the original book now unobtainable, these are illustrations considered necessary to the completeness of this present volume.

It would be impossible to consider producing a book containing a large number of photographs without the valued contributions afforded by colleagues, institutions, friends and interested well wishers. It is here that I gratefully acknowledge the enthusiastic help, support and assistance given by the following:

Hampshire County Museums Service
Colleagues and friends at Havant Museum and Portsmouth City Museums and Records Office
The Imperial War Museum
The *News* Portsmouth
Mr Glyndwr G. Jones
Graham Soffe
Ralph Cousins
Mr T. Short
Mr T. Taussik
David Jordan
Betty Marshall
Peter Barge
Arthur Ricketts
Audrey Rogers
Russell Fox
Peter Newberry
Noel and Valerie Pycroft
Muriel Hudson
Alan Bell
Kathleen Hollingsbee

I am particularly indebted to Ilse McKee, for allowing me access to her late husband's personal notes, detailing incidents recorded throughout his very active, adventurous life and, for permitting the reproduction of photographs from the McKee family albums.

To Nicola Bennett, for her willingness to assist by providing photographs and information relating to the Marshall family, of which she is a descendant, I also owe a particular debt of thanks.

Finally and in no small measure, I acknowledge Nicholas Danby of the Seacourt Tennis Club for his enthusiasm in delving into the archives of both the club and the Marshall family and producing for me, a wealth of photographic evidence from the earliest years. Whilst every possible effort has been made to determine ownership or copyright of the illustrations within these pages, I ask forgiveness if I have unwittingly transgressed in my use of the very few examples whose origins are, in fact, unknown.

For the benefit of readers who would wish to further pursue the necessarily brief historical descriptions and commentaries contained within these pages, they are invited to visit the Havant Museum in East Street where they can, in the Local Studies and Resources Room, browse at their leisure among the comprehensive collection of maps, books, documents, photographs and news cuttings. Copies of Havant Parish Registers both in book form and fiche are also available.

Introduction

ORIGINS

Until the introduction of the Local Government Act of 1894, Havant, Hayling and Langstone had been districts within the ancient Hundred of Bosmere, a system of local government introduced into southern counties of Britain probably in the tenth century. A further confusion of titles, this time concerning the county, existed until the first of April 1959 when the County Council agreed that the name of the administrative county should be changed from the County of Southampton to that of Hampshire. Hayling Island in Hampshire, is part of the Borough of Havant, its northern shore lying just 2 miles south of the Havant town centre and, literally, little more than a stone's throw from the old village of Langstone, through which one must pass if approaching the island from the mainland.

Havant, Langstone and Hayling are located almost on the Hampshire/West Sussex border, with nearby Emsworth actually divided between both counties. The eastern shoreline of Hayling Island is, in places, a matter of just a few yards from where the county boundary passes through Chichester Harbour. Nearby Thorney Island is entirely within the County of West Sussex. To the northwest of both Havant and Hayling, the skyline is dominated by the Portsdown Hill while to the south, across the Solent, the higher ground of the Isle of Wight combines with that of the Portsdown to give a modicum of protection in the extremes of weather which would otherwise affect this southeast corner of Hampshire. Hayling's geographical position on the south coast gives it an enviable record high in the league tables of British sunshine figures.

Nowhere in Hampshire are there to be found the chalk cliffs which are a feature of many parts of Britain's south coast, unless one considers the Portsdown. To those of us who are familiar with the local geography, this 7-mile-long outlyer of the South Downs, forms a natural backdrop to our coastal harbours and settlements. We must however, transport ourselves back in time for many millions of years and understand that the immense primeval forces involved in continental drift and which created the mountain ranges of Europe, were also responsible for the formation of the

South Downs. Fluctuations in sea levels coupled with continuous lifting and folding of the land masses are today evident in the several ancient beach formations on the south face of the Portsdown. Raised Beach deposits are known to geologists at Cams (Fareham), Downend (Portchester), Paulsgrove Pit and at the exposed chalk of Farlington Redoubt; proof indeed that today's Portsdown Hill had earlier been a cliff mass facing and subjected to, the vagaries of a prehistoric sea; a sea that covered much of Great Britain, including what we now know to be Hayling Island.

Projecting forward in geological time to a suggested 10,000 years ago, the question may be posed: where at this time was Hampshire's southern shore? We do know that the Isle of Wight was part of the land mass coupled to present-day Dorset and that the 'so called' Solent River divided the Isle of Wight from Hampshire before reaching the sea at some point near Selsey. An impression of this ancient land and seascape may yet be experienced by ascending the Portsdown, looking south, and absorbing the panorama from east to west (Selsey and beyond to Southampton and beyond). Admiralty charts of the mid-nineteenth century show the hill to be 414 feet at maximum height, although the vista may be appreciated from almost any point along its 7-mile length. The view confronting the reader is of a partially flooded coastal plain extending for perhaps 50 or more miles east to west, a plain which includes the Gosport Peninsula, Portsea Island, Hayling Island, Thorney Island and the Selsey Peninsula. Prior to the melt waters which accompanied the last glaciation, it is known that this entire coastal plain was dry land interspersed with occasional streams and rivers feeding the Solent River and inhabited by creatures known today only in tropical regions of the world. What then happened to create the land and seascape with which we are familiar?

Towards the end of the last ice-age, much of Britain was covered by an ice sheet with melt water rushing steadily seaward. The result being the raising of sea levels and the drowning of the Solent River valley which was then to become today's Solent and Spithead. The relatively higher ground of this, by now, coastal plain, formed the islands, land masses and harbours that we know today. This higher ground remains, however, only just above mean high water and with the known effects of global warming, it seems inevitable that, at some time in the distant future, the sea will once again encroach upon our southern shores. It is likely that the lesser islands in the three harbours of Portsmouth, Langstone and Chichester – for example Pewit, Binness, Fowley and Pilsey – will be among the first to be swallowed, followed by the Farlington Marshlands which are barely above the present high water levels. An indication of the seriousness of the situation is perhaps more fully understood when we consider that a survey of 1587 shows Selsey to have been an island at that time and that sections of the adjoining coast, fortified against possible Spanish incursion have, together with their cannon, long since surrendered to the sea. That Hayling has also suffered a loss of its land mass is undeniable. Documentary evidence from at least the Middle Ages is irrefutable. The evidence of marine archaeology gained in recent years, has also added substance to what had previously been part speculation. The supposed existence of a lost settlement together with its church, submerged two miles south of Hayling must now be taken seriously. The more recent claim that the remains of a Roman harbour may exist off the northeast shore of the Isle of Wight must also be considered, as must the assertion that Hayling once stretched as far south as the Nab Shoal.

Whilst scholars, historians and archeologists continue to disagree as to the validity or indeed location of the mythical Hayling Island sites, local legends, handed down for generations, together with the hard evidence of materials raised from both Hayling Bay and Langstone Harbour, remain within the folklore of the Islanders. That Hayling has oft' times changed its dimensions and that acres have been lost to the sea, cannot be argued. The evidence is there... the reader is prevailed upon again to visit the Portsdown, to take a long look upon the coastal plain, see Hayling Island in its now familiar setting and allow the mind to drift over many millennia, visualising all the while, the many scenic changes that have taken place.

Langstone village has contributed substantially to the history of the district and has always been the stepping-off point for those wishing to visit Hayling Island. With its origins set in prehistoric times, the Wadeway had, until 1824, provided the only method of reaching the Island (unless by boat), for it was in that year that the first ever bridge was opened for both pedestrian and vehicular traffic.

Depending on the state of the tide, it had been possible to transport oneself, carts and / or livestock, using the Wadeway from the Langstone shore to Hayling

although, as its name suggests, it was probable that the journey was often accomplished by wading for much of the way! Coinciding roughly with the construction of the bridge, the course of the Wadeway was permanently interrupted when a deep water channel was cut through it to allow passage of barge traffic on the new London to Portsmouth Waterway via Chichester and Langstone Harbours. The village of Langstone is said to have derived its name from the Saxon 'Longstone' and buried somewhere in the shoreline mud is an erratic boulder, the Longstone, one of many such stones jettisoned 100,000 years ago from a prehistoric ice floe that 'seeded' the local district; Hayling has examples still to be seen throughout the Island. In 1980, the historical importance of Langstone was recognised when an embossed plaque was placed on the restored quay, listing those authorities, institutions and national companies who, by their combined financial efforts, had made the restoration possible.

Langstone Quay

Langstone was an acknowledged port in former times. Upon occasions of general levy and the issue of 'ships orders', the town of Havant furnished from its port of Langstone – 'one ship of war properly equipped for the defence of the realm'. Latterly, the port was much used in the trade of grain, coal, shingle and fertilizer by the various sailing barges which became known as 'Langstone Barges'.

Restoration of the Quay and its surrounds was made possible in 1980 with funds provided by:

Havant Borough Council
Sainsbury Charitable Fund
Hampshire County Council
Whitbread Wessex Ltd
Civic Trust
G.Gale & Co. Ltd
Chichester Harbour Conservancy
Southern Tourist Board

Of the two local harbours, Chichester Harbour takes its name from the City of Chichester, the County Town of West Sussex and, in addition to the island of Thorney, is also home to the tiny islands of Fowley and Pilsey. Langstone Harbour, however, is named, incongruously perhaps, after the shoreline village. Within Langstone Harbour are to be found the several Binness Islands. Once popular as picnic locations for the boating fraternity, they are now designated bird sanctuaries with access forbidden to the public at large. At some time in the distant past, these lesser islands must have been easily accessed or were, perhaps, isolated dry areas within the marshlands; each of them having revealed considerable evidence that man was a frequent visitor with the discovery of his flint tools, arrow heads and so on. A funerary urn containing cremated human remains has also been discovered in the nearby mud-lands giving rise to the belief that the Binness Islands have been used by generations of our ancestors from the Paleolithic to the Bronze Age and beyond.

The origins of the word 'Hayling' are not so clear cut and obvious as perhaps that suggested for Langstone; documents dating from the year 956 until the present day, give at least twenty varying ways of spelling Hayling, from the 'Heglingaigai' of the Saxon Charters to the now accepted version dating from the eighteenth Century. The Saxon dictionaries define 'Ing' as meaning 'the people of' and to quote from Eilert Ekwall's *Oxford Dictionary of English Place Names*, 'Hayling Island is the island of Haelinga's or Haegel's people'. Hayling Island has produced a great deal of evidence of the presence of early man, far more so in fact than neighbouring Portsmouth. It would seem that Hayling was perhaps easier to reach from the mainland or that it offered more in the way of wildlife and other primitive food sources to sustain the early inhabitants. Whatever the reasons, it was obviously necessary at some period to defend these people and their assets; the Tournerbury Ring at the eastern side of the Island (comparable with our ancient hill forts / enclosures) bears witness to the fact that invaders were a constant threat to the community.

The Saxon peoples considered all islands to be holy places and we the British, members of an island race, have always been enviously looked upon by foreign intruders who would usurp our lands and way of life. That the threat was apparent even in those far off days of our pre-history, readily brings to mind the fears of an invasion by a foreign power in our recent lifetime, and that the shores of Hayling Island were once again defended. Evidence still remains of these prehistoric defences as does evidence of the defences of the Second World War.

The pictorial content of this book will enlarge upon these and other themes and, with its illustrations, advance the reader from those very early times through to the closing years of the twentieth century.

Hayling is an enigma, an island of questionable legends and disputed facts. It is a truism that most, if not all islands, possess an air of isolation coupled with an indefinable 'something' which mainlanders, try as they may, fail to penetrate or understand.

MAP OF HAYLING ISLAND.

The Archaeology of Hayling Island

For very many years farmers had been troubled by the profusion of stone which, lying beneath the surface, had damaged plough shares and inhibited growth of seasonal crops in the Touncil Field. The stones together with infrequent finds of a suggested Roman origin prompted Mr Talfourd Ely of University College London to investigate the location. Working entirely alone and spurning all offers of help, he excavated the whole site between 1897 and 1907.

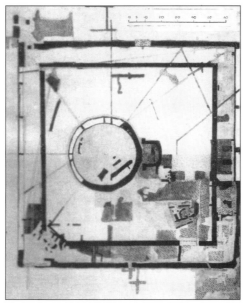

Talfourd Ely finally ceased his explorations in 1907 at the age of sixty-six years. His site plan drawn up in 1908 shows he excavated an area approximately 130 ft by 140 ft, recording as he progressed each aspect and every individual 'find' discovered. Summing up the ten years spent here he wrote, 'The few rustics who approached spoke of my seeking "a crock of gold"; the treasure really sought and gained was health, strength of body and the pleasures of the mind'.

Aerial photographs recorded during the severe drought of 1976 revealed a stunning series of crop marks in the Touncil Field; marks which closely tallied with those sketched and described by Talfourd Ely whose work, largely disregarded by later archaeologists, was now acknowledged to be more accurate than supposed.

Photograph by Grahame Soffe

A three year series of excavations confirmed that here were the remains of a Romano-British Temple.

Approaching the end of these excavations, an appeal was made for volunteers to assist in all aspects of the work; anyone able to wield a pick axe or take on the more delicate work of cleaning and washing specimens or able to help in any other capacity were recruited; volunteers arrived from London University, Canada, Australia, Poland and locally from Havant College.

The site was finally opened to public viewing at weekends during September/October 1978. A visit to the area today will reveal nothing of the excitement generated during a three year exploration of the field; an archaeological adventure second only in local importance to that of the Roman Palace at Fishbourne.

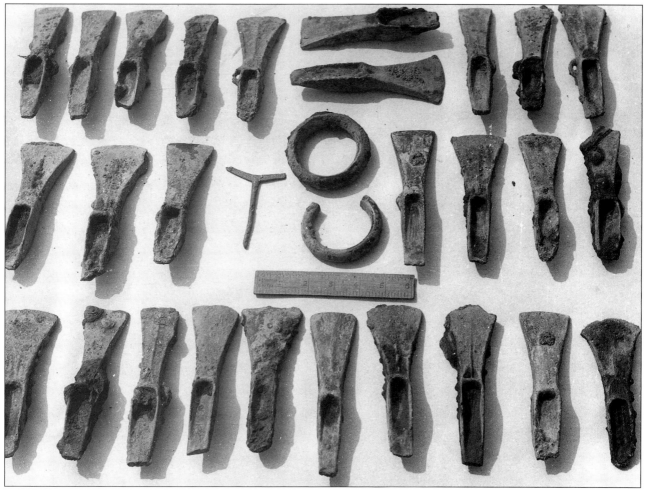

Known as the Gable Head Hoard, this magnificent collection was discovered in August 1957 when drainage workers were employing a mechanical digger in Elm Close. The entire hoard consisting of twenty-seven bronze palstaves, two bracelets, one of which is incomplete, and a fragment of a quoit headed pin are currently part of the City of Portsmouth Museum's collection.

Evidence of the founder's craft, again including palstaves, has also been found in the grounds of H.M.S. *Sultan* in Gosport, St James' Hospital Portsmouth and, coincidentally, St Mary's Hospital Portsmouth. The splendid hoard pictured here, however, is yet another Hayling find. Unearthed in December 1995 by caring metal detector enthusiasts Nick Goring and John Walbridge, the find was not made at the same location as the 1957 discovery. This collection is currently displayed in the Havant Museum.

Hayling Island continues to produce occasional, random finds of historical interest such as this restored, almost globular, jar discovered in 1955. A giant example of its type approximately 20 inches in height with four diametrically opposed lugs around the neck. Made of a coarse reddish ware it is thought to be late Bronze or early Iron Age in origin. It is currently in the City of Portsmouth Museum's collection.

In the autumn of 1997, this most unusual stone was trawled from the seabed at a point in Hayling Bay approaching the entrance to Chichester Harbour. Curious as to its origin or purpose, the finder Mr T. Short submitted it for classification to the Hampshire Museums Service. Of approximately 18 inches in length with a crudely worked groove around its centre, it is thought to have been a primitive anchor. Probably secured by a form of hide rope, it is almost certainly prehistoric; its loss would have represented a minor catastrophe for the owner.

Langstone, Village and Harbour

Langston Road, Havant.

Langstone Road Havant 1915. The toll gate at the nearby Hayling bridge together with the local railway crossing were responsible for the massive traffic jams experienced with the growing popularity of the motor car and the discovery of the Island as a holiday resort. Gardens of the houses in this road have sometimes yielded pottery and building fragments associated with the Roman Villa in Langstone Avenue.

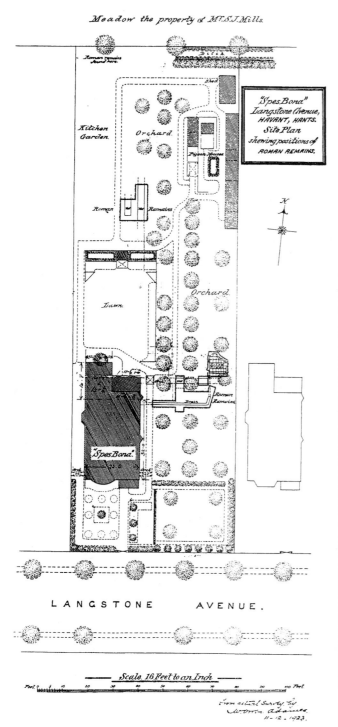

In 1923 Mr W. Owen Adames of Langstone Avenue noticed that his small orchard had failed to bear fruit for yet another season. An investigation of the soil suggested that buried debris was responsible for the lack of growth and stunted appearance.

Evidence was soon forthcoming when the garden was dug to a depth of 2 feet.

The removal of more top soil revealed a considerable section of tiled flooring.

These early excavations were incorporated into a new garden feature using
many stones from an original Roman building.

Work to reveal yet more of the now confirmed Roman Villa continued until 1927. Most interesting perhaps was the hypocaust system of heating shown in this obviously posed photograph. To encourage visitor access and to preserve the find, Mr Adames had a viewing platform erected over this section of the site.

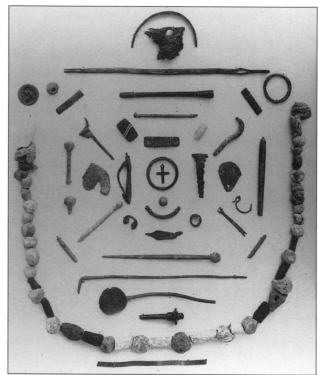

Suggestions that the location had been inhabited from perhaps prehistoric times were confirmed when, from the lower levels, flint tools and weapons, and a necklace made entirely from pieces of bone, chalk and hollow stones were unearthed. A British coin dating from approximately 150 B.C. was also discovered.

Metal items from the Roman period are displayed here together with the neck section of a jug and two pieces of worked bone.

That the site was inhabited by the Romans and, perhaps, by the Saxons for a suggested several hundred years or more, is evidenced by the large amount of fragmented and discarded pottery and tiles exhibited in the 'Aladdin's Cave' which was the Adames' garden shed.

Three of the Adames' daughters, again in a posed photograph, are surrounded by hundreds, if not thousands of finds made on the site. Of particular interest is the chalk block seen bottom left: It features a design of unknown significance. (See illustration below).

Accurately reproduced in a contemporary sketch is the curious design of the previous photograph. The question asked then and now; is it Roman, Saxon or even perhaps early British? It is not recorded at which level the block was found.

With crossing gates closed to road traffic, a train is approaching Langstone Station from Havant c. 1930. The wooden platform pictured here was later replaced by a concrete structure in 1950.

Alf Harris Collection

LANGSTONE STATION.

The 'Terrier' tank engine *Knowle* was used on the Havant to Hayling line during various stages of its long life. Built in 1880, it is thought to have still been in service locally at the closure of the line in 1963.

Each affectionately known as the 'Hayling Billy', the several 'Terrier' tank engines were much loved by all who knew them. This commercial post-card conveys a lighthearted impression of the local attitude toward the trains and should not be taken seriously. The message written on the reverse of the card in 1913 however says, 'Down here for the weekend, unfortunately I have to travel by the "caterpillar" in the picture!'

A date of 1881 has been confirmed for this photograph of the Langstone windmill. How did this little group manage to keep their feet or indeed make their way to the shore in conditions such as this?

Langstone's windmill and water-mill were sited adjacent to each other on the shoreline. Fed by the Lymbourne springs, it is supposed that the millpond waters could have also been partly tidal, the sea being only yards distant. Following restoration both properties have been converted into living accommodation.

Both mills were retired from active use in the late nineteenth century following the introduction of modern mechanical methods of milling and the undoubted expense of maintaining the old plant.

The old Mill, Langston, Havant.

Strategically sited near the shore at Langstone and protected from high tides by a substantial wall, the property seen here was built as a look-out station for H.M. Coastguard in the mid nineteenth century. Commanding spectacular views over the local waters and seaward approaches to the village, the house together with its tower is still called 'The Lookout' and has provided enviable family accommodation since 1925.

Pictured from the tower of the previous photograph, this idyllic scene shows the buildings which once housed both the wind- and water-mills together with the 'Royal Oak' public house.

On a postcard dated 1912, the scene is of cattle being led through Langstone High Street from the shore after taking a short cut from pastures which lay along the coast on the Warblington side of Langstone.

In November 1914, members of the Stent Family released their home 'Langstone Towers' for use as a Red Cross Auxiliary Military Hospital. It remained as such until January 1919 having treated 1430 patients. Posing for the group photograph on an unknown date, are uniformed patients and staff. Military hospital patients wore a blue flannel suit, the coat collar having white facings, white shirt and red tie. This mode of dress was compulsory through and beyond both world wars, the author having been so fitted out in 1946! A fuller description with facts and figures concerning this establishment is recorded in part three of 'The Making of Havant' and may be consulted in the Havant Museum Local Studies Room or the Public Libraries.

Both the Langstone shoreline and that of North Hayling are viewed in this aerial photograph of the 1930s. Following the closure of the railway in 1963, the bridge on the right was removed. The road bridge on the left was the original timber construction of 1824, remaining in use until September 1958 when the present concrete structure was opened. It is just possible to see on the extreme left of the picture, part of the centuries-old Wadeway which had provided the only access to Hayling prior to 1824.

Legend has it that in the years following the First World War, a captured German submarine was bought to Langstone to be broken up. This local 'folk tale' persisted until 1997, when a collection of family snapshots was donated to Havant Museum. Among them was the photograph featured here. The vessel is seen east of the two Langstone bridges lying at low tide, a short distance from the shore. The photograph has been examined by experts at the Royal Naval Submarine Museum at Gosport and, from the number displayed on its conning tower, plus the configuration of its hull design etc., has been declared to be a British vessel, submarine No. F2. The Navy had three such craft built to an Italian Fiat Laurenti design; F2 was constructed by Whites Shipbuilders of Cowes in the Isle of Wight. The innovative design was a failure however and each vessel was condemned to the breakers' yard. F2 was purchased by Mr C. Welton of Portsmouth, towed to Langstone and dismantled for its scrap value.

Arriving at this point from the mainland, all vehicles were obliged to pay a toll. As the original wooden bridge could not accommodate heavy loads, bus passengers had to walk across, rejoining their transport at the other end. Likewise, petrol tankers delivering fuel to island garages had to be of a smaller capacity and of a lesser weight than those in general use, thus restricting the quantity of petrol which could be delivered to any one location. This photograph, however, shows a Pratt's Oil Company vehicle making a delivery of petrol in two-gallon cans. Older readers will recall motor spirit being sold by this method at garages before the introduction of calibrated and approved petrol pumps and underground storage tanks.

Hayling road bridge c.1935 seen from the north shore of the Island. The Ship Inn at Langstone Village is in the distance.

Following in the steps of the local sailing and fisher folk who had organised and enjoyed annual sailing and rowing events from at least the early years of the twentieth century, a number of enthusiasts made the decision to form a sailing club in Langstone Village. With the Second World War recently over and restrictions on sailing activities relaxed, the need for suitable premises became the immediate priority. The first hurdle was overcome when, at a meeting held in the bar of the The Ship Inn, the landlord, Albert Cobb, offered the embryo club the use of an old malting room. The photograph c.1945 records a happy gathering of members in this their first club room.

An annual regatta is part of the social scene at the Langstone Sailing Club and this picture shows that visiting craft accepted an invitation to visit and perhaps compete in the events. The vessel seen centre is *Tarka*, owned and sailed by Les Hudson. This vessel commenced life as a rescue craft which could be dropped from an aircraft to aid 'ditched' aircrews who had the misfortune to crash or bale-out into the sea.

The reader could be forgiven for perhaps confusing, at first sight, this vessel with the early chain ferry which linked Portsmouth with Gosport; not so however, for the craft pictured here is the paddle steamer *Carrier*. Originally employed north of the border on the River Tay, it was brought to Langstone where from 1885 until 1888, it provided a service between Langstone and Brading in the Isle of Wight. The first and only example of a train ferry from the mainland to the Island, it will be seen to have transported coal trucks to the Island's railway network for onward distribution.

Courtesy of Alan Bell

The 1000 foot-long railway bridge, a minor triumph of Victorian engineering, was supported on wooden piles driven into the seabed. The timbers were later encased in concrete, and it is these concrete blocks which remain today as the only visible evidence that a railway ever passed this way.

The railway bridge is shown again with its centre span opened to allow the movement of shipping between Chichester and Langstone harbours. A 30 foot gap could be created as in this instance which involved the through passage of a sailing barge.

This photograph, taken in February 1963, is an important addition to our local archives. In a memorably severe winter, parts of Langstone Harbour froze over for almost two weeks. At low water, mudlands are seen covered in ice whilst the Havant to Hayling train makes its way across the frozen channel. Boats moored in the harbour became trapped in the surface ice and, together with their mooring blocks drifted with the ice, out of the harbour on the outgoing tide. One of the larger craft to go missing (later to be recovered at Spithead), was the *Esso Langstone*, a refuelling vessel permanently moored in mid-stream and used by fishing and pleasure craft. At low water it was said to be possible to walk on the ice floes from the Milton shore to the Eastney Ferry Road. It was later in this same year that the Hayling train service was discontinued, making its final journey on the 2 November.

Reproduced by permission of the *Portsmouth News*

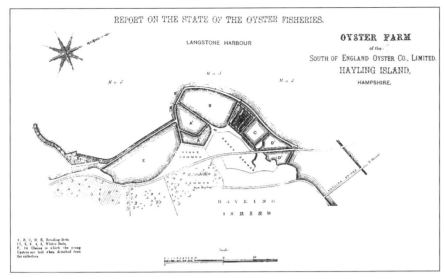

The largest oyster complex on the island was established by the South of England Oyster Company Limited in about 1880 and comprised the extensive beds pictured in this site drawing of approximately that date. The farm covered many acres reclaimed from the sea and provided pens (beds) for oysters during varying stages of growth.

The extent and boundaries of the North Hayling Oyster Farm can be appreciated in this aerial view of c. 1980. The nineteenth century developers were responsible for bringing to the site the many hundreds of tons of soil and hardcore needed to establish the extensive bund walls which surrounded and divided the breeding beds... all this in the sea and at varying states of the tide! The industry alas is no more and the Hayling Oyster, once a delicacy exported and enjoyed nationwide, is now a rare creature and, if found, because of the pollution of our harbours, is eaten at your own risk!

Peter Williams Collection

Oyster beds had been established in the harbour as early as 1819, when Matthew Russell took a lease on this tiny island close to the mainland in the upper reaches of the harbour. The property pictured, served as his residence and watch house to safeguard the oyster beds laid down in Crastick's Channel (later known as Russell's Lake); oyster poaching being an activity common at that time. Damaged by war-time bombing and later demolished, the house during its near one hundred-and-fifty-years existence was variously known as The Oyster House, The Lone House, The Black House and Russell's House. Members of the Russell family, each of them involved in the shell-fish industry, also owned the house now named The Winkle Market in Langstone High Street and two properties near the shore at Milton Locks on the Portsmouth side of the harbour.

Shingle has been gathered from the Winner Banks and sundry locations in and around Hayling Bay for many generations. Sailing barges were the means of collecting and transporting the material for perhaps a hundred years until the arrival of the steam and motor vessels of the twentieth century. Unloading a cargo of shingle at its berth in Store House Lake Langstone Harbour, is *The City of Portsmouth.*

Photograph by Glyndwr G. Jones

A familiar sight in Langstone Harbour for more than one year, the barquentine *Eolus* spent much of her enforced stay berthed at Heaver's quay on the Portsmouth shore. Originally a Baltic trader of 386 tons, the vessel had been converted to a square rigger. She left Langstone Harbour at Christmas 1973 to embark on 'a round the world holiday of a lifetime '. Suffering many misfortunes; a change of ownership and a change of name to the *Black Pearl*, she tragically sank in Malta's Grand Harbour. The last news report of the ' ship that died of shame ' was in 1978 when she still lay rotting in that harbour.

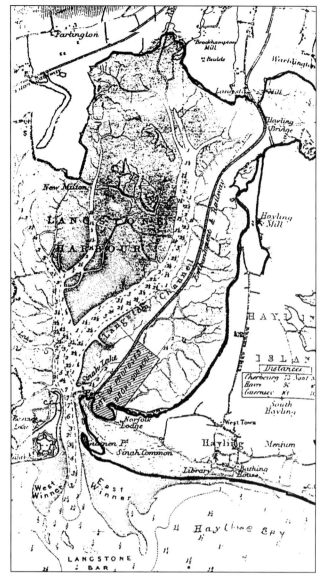

Plans for the development of Langstone Harbour have taken many forms, each of them being thought sensible, practicable and desirable in their day. Here, a map dated 1855 shows a proposed area of docklands amounting to 200 acres with rail connections, to be established in Langstone Harbour on Hayling's west coastline. With Fort Cumberland on the Eastney shore and a Martello Tower on the Hayling shore, a defended commercial harbour could have been established here in complete contrast to the naval, Portsmouth Harbour.

Across the water in neighbouring Portsmouth, plans were implemented in 1837 to create a 220 acre system of docks wharves and bonded warehouses in Langstone Harbour, also served by a railway connection. The scheme which was later abandoned, included access via a canal from a point near Southsea Common, this time to provide a harbour principally for Britain's colonial trade. The co-operation of the colonies was sought but it was eventually found that the colossal cost of the undertaking precluded its adoption.

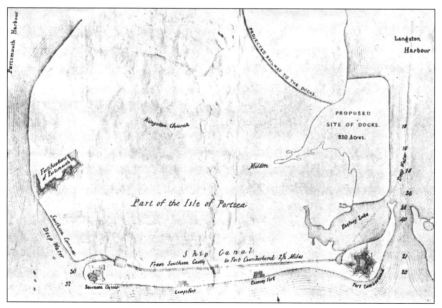

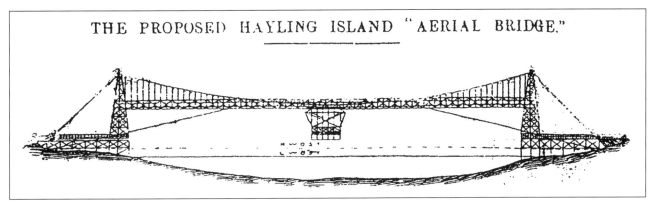

THE PROPOSED HAYLING ISLAND "AERIAL BRIDGE."

In April 1903, the *Portsmouth Evening News* published this illustration together with details of a proposed Aerial Bridge to link Hayling Island with Portsmouth and Southsea from West Beach to the Eastney peninsula. The bridge was to have a span of 720 feet and carry a 'car' with perhaps three to four carriages capable of carrying pedestrians and cyclists up to the weight of 60 tons while, should it be required for troops, 5000 could be conveyed from one side to the other in the course of one hour! In the event, at a meeting of Hayling Parish Council in June 1903, the proposals were totally rejected and, almost one hundred years later, we are still reliant on a ferry link to connect the two shores.

The Ferry Hayling Island.

The Spithead Series.

The wide sweep of the Island shoreline is, today, the scene of great activity, particularly in the summer season when sailors, fisherman, sail boarders and all manner of holiday and marine activities are catered for from this area. This part of the harbour and coastline would have been denied to the future public if, of course, the plans of the 1855 harbour had reached fruition.

An aerial photograph from the 1950s reveals almost all of the southern edge of the Island. The stark wilderness of Sinah Common together with the inland sand dunes shows this side of the Island to be virtually uninhabited. The Kench, a small, natural, protected harbour was, at this time, a haven for a number of houseboats, most of which were former naval patrol boats, M.T.B's, and landing craft, each sold surplus to requirements following the Second World War. After conversion, they proved to be comfortable homes at a time when the national housing shortage was at its most acute. This, the western edge of the Island, is served by a ferry to and from Portsmouth; the pontoon landing stage is pictured to the left of the plinths on which the Mulberry Harbour units were constructed.

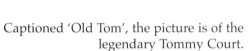

Of the several Hayling ferry boats employed over the years, the *Sinah* pictured here, is a vessel whose origins are thought to have been that of a ships' lifeboat. A photograph of the mid-1930s sees the craft approaching Hayling pontoon, its coxswain almost certainly Tom Court.

Captioned 'Old Tom', the picture is of the legendary Tommy Court.

A much later addition to the ferry company, this vessel also bears the name
Sinah and is pictured leaving the Eastney pontoon in June 1967.

By 1994, the ferry company had taken possession of the *Pride of Hayling*. Berthed at Hayling, the Portsmouth shoreline provides the background.

Photograph by Glyndwr G. Jones

The Island Scene

Oakdene Cottage in the Havant Road , must be a contender for the 'oldest building' title on the Island; certainly it is possibly the most attractive. Believed to date from the sixteenth century, D.I.Y. work carried out by enthusiastic owners over several years, has revealed pottery from the seventh century, a coin from the eleventh century, a mediaeval axe head and re-used Roman building materials probably taken from the remains of a nearby Roman Temple in the Touncil Field.

49 – Stoke, Hayling Island.

The Stoke Village smithy pictured in 1912, though in a neglected state, still remains attached to Forge Cottage on the corner of Copse Lane. Meanwhile a memorial inscription recorded in St Mary's Churchyard in 1922 quotes a tombstone epitaph which may perhaps relate to the village blacksmith of Stoke ?

'My sledge and hammer lie reclined
my bellows too have lost their wind
my fire's extinct my forge decayed
and in dust my vice is laid
my coal is spent my iron gone
my nails are drove my work is done.'

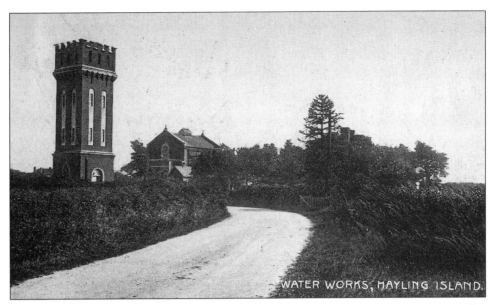

In 1895, the South Hayling Water Company Limited, undertook to supply the southern half of the Island with piped water, the source being a well at Stoke. A pumping house and water tower were constructed and, shortly after in 1898, the supply was extended to include the remainder of the Island. With continued local development, Havant Rural District Council arranged, in 1924, for the supply to be provided from Bedhampton by the Portsmouth Water Company and trunk mains were installed. The water tower, so long a local landmark, was demolished in 1952; the pump house remaining until the 1980s.

The village of Stoke is possibly Hayling's oldest continuously inhabited settlement. Burials discovered on the common and seashore are among the most ancient known on the Island. The buildings seen here are still to be found at what is the most hazardous bend on the Island roads.

Bidden & Co., were the last active brewers in Havant. Here the drayman is making a delivery to the Yew Tree Inn at Stoke Village, Hayling.

Hayling's Manor House was built in 1777 by the then Duke of Norfolk on an ancient, moated site which has a history dating back many centuries to at least the Norman period. A theory seriously considered is that the location is that of the Island's lost priory.

Charles M. Clarke, the long serving vicar of Hayling (1889-1938), is pictured with Eleanor his second wife. Upon his death in 1938, Eleanor had the ancient Pound in Manor Road rebuilt and a commemorative plaque placed there as a lasting memorial to a much loved husband and respected parish priest.

Titled 'The Pound, South Hayling', the photograph is of the junction of Church and Manor Roads. The remains of the original Pound are not within the fenced enclosure in the centre of the scene but remain hidden, amid the trees, on the right of the picture.

'Granny' King is seen at the door of her cottage in Higworth Lane; the date, unfortunately, is not known but believed to be c.1920. The tiny cottage is constructed of cob, a mixture of unbaked clay and straw. This type of dwelling, inexpensive to build and once common in rural areas, may still be found today in many third-world countries.

This scene, recorded in 1915, shows Manor Road as a country lane. Widened and having a tarmacadam surface, this thoroughfare now carries perhaps fifty per cent of the Island's traffic.

A later, 1930's view of Manor Road, shows it still to be part of rural Hayling with hayricks and farm buildings bordering the footpath.

HAM FARM, HAYLING ISLAND.

The junction of Manor and Station Roads is the setting for this photograph. Called Manor Farm, it later became known as Manor and Ham Farm. Several 'hands off' campaigns have been staged over the years to protect the diminishing farmlands at Hayling from development. A modern public house, the Barley Mow, now occupies this site with adjoining fields giving way to modern housing.

William Padwick's dream of Hayling Island rivalling both Cheltenham and Bath is visualised in the print reproduced here. Commissioned by Padwick, and executed by architect and civil engineer Joseph A. Barsley, the print is representative of the 'New Town Project', planned for the south beach of the Island.

Extravagantly large houses were built and others planned, to accommodate the wealthy who were by now, attracted by the promise of 'Utopia by the sea'. Ammenities to be provided included the Library pictured here.

Cafe and Pony Stand, Hayling Island.

Standing isolated on the shore, the Library later became part of a different holiday scene when summer visitors came to the Island en-masse. The once elegant building now provided refreshments, ices and seaside novelties as well as becoming a base for the popular pony and donkey rides.

Chateau Blanc Girls School, South Hayling

The largest private residence on the Island and indeed, the most impressive, was Westfield, the home of the Sandeman family. The building suffered the first of several changes of use and name, when it became the Grand Hotel and later still, the Chateau Blanc Girls School. Its next title was St Patrick's Open Air School with a final name change being assumed in 1980 when it adopted its final role as The Choir School of Our Lady and Saint John. A Hayling landmark since the 1830s, the building was demolished in 1993. A small part of the rear block remains however as a rest home for the elderly; an estate of modern houses occupies the once attractive gardens.

The Crescent, Hayling Island.

Similarities between the Crescent at South Hayling and those at Bath, Cheltenham and Brighton were purely intentional when the terrace was erected in 1825. The Regency architecture of the ten houses comprising the terrace is undisputedly elegant, but curiously unsymmetrical, from which, one may assume that the Crescent was never completed. The principal dwelling in the row was 'Norfolk House' which explains why, even today, the terrace is often referred to as Norfolk Crescent.

The Royal Hotel was yet another 1825 addition to the New Town development. Holiday brochures of the day highlighted the fact that the principal rooms commanded magnificent views of the Solent, Isle of Wight and the ever changing panorama of passing shipping. A recent conversion of the building into luxury apartments has prompted the agents to again emphasise the scenic advantages of living in this popular and much sought-after location.

Hoping to promote and encourage the 'Sport of Kings' at Hayling, a race meeting was staged here in front of, and beyond, the Royal Hotel and Crescent in July 1867. A grandstand was built facing the hotel and, with the exception of perhaps half-a-mile hidden behind Mr Harris's Farm, the entire course of 2 miles could be viewed from the grandstand.

Racing programme 1867, first day.

Racing programme 1867, second day.

The popularity of the seaside is becoming apparent although in the early years, modesty precluded all but the most daring to don a swim suit. A suggested date for this photograph is 1918.

For years a holiday retreat for the retired and the wealthy, the Island was inevitably discovered by the masses in the early 1930s. Safe sandy beaches together with other seasonal amenities, encouraged family groups to visit and perhaps holiday on the Island. Here a Punch and Judy Man provides the entertainment.

The popularity of the motor car (and motor cycle) is beginning to influence the holiday scene as witnessed in this pre-war postcard. The old Library building with its neo-classic facade has, by this time, been converted into a, not so typical, seaside tea room.

The establishment of a traditional seaside fairground c.1934, provided an additional holiday attraction. The Grand Hotel (previously Westfield House) is the large building in the background.

As the Island grew in popularity as a holiday resort, guide books extolling its virtues and publicizing its facilities were published. The following advertisements come from one such guide which appeared in 1930.

'Monkey Island' features in many postcard views of Hayling. A most unusual and novel attraction in the years prior to the Second World War, the man-made centre-piece of the fairground was home to a colony of monkeys who were confined to their rock by the presence of the water filled boating pool. A number of the inhabitants are active in this picture including the bold member of the clan who sits upon the miniature clock tower.

Although the boating pool survived the war years, the Monkey Island suffered from neglect and vandalism resulting in its demolition and removal.

This location is exactly that of the present fairground and also that of the Monkey Island of the previous two pictures. In this photograph, c. 1910, the tents are probably those erected for the camps of the military whose summer exercises brought them to Hayling.

A regular form of entertainment for locals and a source of interest for holiday makers, the arrival on shore of the returning fisherman could also provide fresh fish for sale at bargain prices.

Sir William (Billy) Butlin opened his first holiday camp at Skegness in 1936. This novel form of holiday entertainment and accommodation was soon to arrive at Hayling when the Civil Service Group established their own camp here. The pictured is dated 1937.

Eastoke Beach and Common were also popular with visitors and day trippers alike. Beach huts placed near the sea provided changing facilities for bathers, protection from inclement weather and a base for al fresco picnics.

Prior to the expansion of the Island as a holiday resort, Eastoke had been a neglected peninsula, wild and undeveloped. Land for building was available, inexpensive and ripe for investment; all factors to encourage the building of reasonably priced, bungalow homes for seasonal or permanent occupation. Considerable numbers of similar properties were quickly erected, so giving the estate the title of 'Bungalow Town'.

Those bungalows built on the south side of the estate bordering the shoreline, were soon to become aware of the hazards to be expected when exposed to high tides and severe onshore gales and, whilst constant and considerable efforts are still pursued to preserve and maintain the shoreline against the ravages of the sea, Nature sometimes proves itself the master, breaching the defences and flooding gardens, properties and surrounding roads.
Upon a shore where the south west wind sets almost continually for nine out of the twelve months of the year. (Longcroft 1857).

The Olive Leaf public house at South Hayling owes its name to that of the Island's first lifeboat which was donated to the service in 1865 by the London Company of Thomas Leaf & Sons. William Goldsmith, the first landlord, was also coxswain of the vessel. The *Olive Leaf* lifeboat, powered by ten oars and Hayling muscle is credited with saving thirty-two lives during its twenty-three years of service with the Hayling Island Station of the R.N.L.I.

The Lifeboat public house is said to have been built at the same time as the Olive Leaf. Tradition tells of the race to complete the buildings and pull the first pint. (We are not told which pub 'won the day'!)

Havant photographer William Scorer was on hand to record this launch of the Hayling lifeboat. The crew, with oars in place, are ready to pull away from the shore once the vessel is cast-off and afloat. Waves breaking in the shallows indicate that worse is to come at sea!

HAYLING ISLAND REGATTA,

MONDAY, AUGUST 25th, 1884.

TO COMMENCE AT ELEVEN O'CLOCK.

Sailing Director : Mr Wm. COAKER, R.N. *Umpire :* Mr J. MARTIN, R.N.

COMMITTEE :—
Wm. GANN, Esq., *Chairman.*

C. J. PARK, Esq.   H. G. KAY, Esq.   W. BODMAN, Esq.
A. E. BRIANT, Esq.   S. P. HUNT, Esq.   J. KILN, Esq.
R. J. KILN, Esq.   A. LEWIS, Esq.

Treasurer : P. M HOUPER, Capital & Counties Bank.

Hon. Sec. : H. R. TRIGG.

OFFICIAL PROGRAMME,

Published by T. SUTER, *West Street, Havant.*

FIRST MATCH —Open Sailing Boats, (fishing boats excluded,) not exceeding 16ft., fixed keel, measured over all. First Prize, £2 2s. Cup.; 2nd ditto, £1; 3rd ditto, 10s. Entrance 2s. 6d. Time allowance, One minute per foot

	NAME.	BELONGING TO	OWNER	FLAG.
1	Edith	Gosport	C. Mountefield	*Red & White triangular & blue diamond*
2	Rose	Gosport	W. Cribb	*red & white perpendicular*
3	Puck		W. D. Gainsford	*blue with yellow grapnell*
4	Young Novel		A. P. Young	*black and yellow*
5	Teneriffe		H. Cribb	*white*
6	Coquette		P. Harris	*red and white Maltese cross*
7	Ellen	Landport	W. Barnett	*blue*

SECOND MATCH.—WESTFIELD CUP, for Yatchs & Pleasure Boats not exceeding 12 tons. Royal Thames Measurement. First Prize, £8 8s. Cup; 2nd ditto, £4 4s. Cup. Entrance 10s. 6d. Time allowed, One minute per ton.

1	Koala	Hayling	H. J. Trigg	*red & white triangles*

The origins of competitive 'club' sailing at Hayling can probably be traced to the regatta of 1884, the programme of which is reproduced here. Of the two present-day Island clubs, that of Mengeham Rythe can be said to consist principally of local sailors, whilst the Hayling Sailing Club based at Sandy Point, attracts a local, national and international membership.

Sail boarding is hardly a spectator sport. It has, however, become the fastest growing water sport enjoyed by solo sailors the world over and the competitiveness of this most recent of water gymnastics, ideally suited to our Solent shores, has made Hayling a principal centre for national and international events. It may well surprise readers to learn, though, that the sport originated here in Hayling Island in 1958 when Peter Chilvers, a schoolboy then aged thirteen years, began experimenting with a piece of plywood, a tent fly sheet and a curtain pole. The results were spectacular and the rest, as they say, is history. Peter eventually went into full-time production of sail boards and even managed to successfully sue the American Windsurfing International over patent infringements.

Peter Williams collection

Golf House, Hayling Island.

Founded by the Sandeman family in 1883, The Hayling Island Golf Club head-quarters were originally housed in what was then, little more than a 'tin and timber' hutment. The growing popularity of the game and the attractions of its unique seaside setting, rapidly demanded the larger, grander, pre-war premises pictured here; premises which ultimately again proved inadequate and were later replaced with the present modern club house.

North Hayling Church.

The twelfth-century St Peter's at Northney, North Hayling, is the oldest surviving church on the Island. Built without foundations, its walls and internal pillars are supported on large 'erratic' boulders, a legacy from the ice-age. As a further means of maintaining the fabric of the ancient building, external buttresses were added in both the thirteenth and fourteenth centuries. St Peter's three bells, cast in about 1350, claim to be the oldest peal in England.

South Hayling Church

It is here in the churchyard of St Mary's South Hayling that a local blacksmith lies buried. Perhaps it is one of the headstones pictured that bears the inscription mentioned earlier in these pages.

Now housed in the Havant Museum, the Hayling stocks and whipping post were previously sited in the churchyard of St Mary's. The humbling of miscreants by public ridicule was the reason for this type of punishment. Prisoners were secured by their ankles and/or wrists; whilst held thus, they were often subjected to abuse both verbal and physical (the throwing of eggs and rotten fruit etc.) by their fellows. A common form of punishment, the stocks were in use nationwide from the middle ages until the reform laws of 1830, when they were considered to be insufficient punishment.

In 1896, Dr J. Lowe recorded the Hayling Yew as being one of the oldest in England. At a height of 4 feet above ground (the recommended height at which a tree should be measured) the girth was 32.4 feet and, assuming that a yew more than 30 foot in girth has been increasing its diameter at a rate of one foot in a century, then this example is more than a thousand years old and was here before the coming of William the Norman!

Oysters have been gathered at Hayling from prehistoric times though it is suggested the Romans were among the first to actually cultivate them. It was during the nineteenth century, however, that a local, commercial industry was established on the Island both at the old Saltings on the east shore and at North Hayling near the railway line. The illustration is of the beds at the Salterns, South Hayling.

Reproduced from a painting by Edward Duncan (1803-1882) is the tide mill at Mill Rythe, Hayling Island. Recorded as early as the thirteenth century, its mechanism was driven by the incoming tide and by waters which had entered and later released from, its tidal millpond. An unsuccessful business venture was conducted at this location in the early years of the twentieth century when a serious attempt was made to extract gold from sea water.

Courtesy of Hampshire County Museums

The sailing barge *Morning Star* lies moored in The Creek (My Lord's Pond) on the Island's east coast; Tournerbury Woods form the background.

'Hollybush House' in Selsmore Road South Hayling, was the home of William Thomas Stead from 1895 to 1912. Journalist and reformer, he drew attention to the practice of purchasing child prostitutes by openly committing the offence himself for which he was imprisoned for three months; his action leading to the Criminal Amendment Act of 1885. Locally and nationally he held meetings and rallies to further the cause of the underprivileged. W. T. Stead lost his life when on passage to America aboard the *Titanic* in 1912.

Photograph by Glyndwr G.Jones

William Thomas Stead is pictured relaxing in the company of a lady whose identity is not known. Perhaps there is on Hayling a reader who may yet identify not only his companion but the Island property with its distinctive brick and tile decoration !

In celebration of Queen Victoria's Diamond Jubilee, W.T.Stead promoted the planting of sixty flowering Chestnut trees in Victoria Avenue, a number of which still remain.

Local celebrations to commemorate the Diamond Jubilee of Queen Victoria in 1897, included the siting of this drinking fountain on the corner of Beach Road and Seafront Road, its inscription reading, 'She brought her people lasting good'.

Just one year following the Queen's Jubilee, the Hotel Victoria opened in Beach Road. In the cinema boom of the 1930s one of the Island's three picture houses, the Victoria, was incorporated into the building.

CHURCH ROAD, HAYLING ISLAND.

Unrecognisable today, but in 1924 the (year of the postcard), Church Road was just one more country road on a quiet unspoiled island.

Tournabury Woods, Hayling Island

Further evidence that Hayling was once an island of country lanes is provided in this 1913 picture postcard of Tournerbury Lane and Woods. In the many commercial cards depicting this and similar scenes, the word Tournerbury (the site of a prehistoric fortified 'ring' camp) is never spelled correctly. Proof indeed that the publishers possessed little or no local knowledge is the fact that this particular card was produced in France!

Church Road continues south as far as Gable Head where the highway then became Elm Grove. The Co-operative store in the picture has been replaced by large modern premises, beyond which all the older buildings have ceased to exist. The present Elm Grove offers a number of shops, fire station, public library, and the Hayling Billy public house.

Elm Grove, Hayling, 1926. Then as now, a principal thoroughfare through the Island. By the mid 1930s, the shop had become Turner's Store and Post Office and, anticipating the holiday trade which was to come, now stocked novelty items, stationery, china and glass.

The principle shopping district on Hayling is at Mengham with a supermarket keeping company with a host of modern stores in stark contrast to the Mengham High Street of the photograph dated 1914. Messrs Seddons, local fish merchants, occupied the 'Black Hut' until the road was redeveloped as a shopping centre in the 1960s.

Contradicting the title of Commercial Road South Hayling, and with much of the flint wall and railings long gone, the location can easily be recognised as South Road. In 1907, the year of the photograph, Hayling had no commercial centre and today, with the exception of the Island Police Headquarters, the road remains purely residential.

Sinah Lane is still a part of the local scene, though now possibly not so remote as depicted in this late Edwardian study.

The Lane will take the traveller through to the Seafront Road, Sinah Common and the golf links; the cottage remains an attractive feature of this minor junction.

Osborne Road (Seafront Road) recorded in 1908, the view looking eastwards. The shop front has yet to receive the balustrade which is a feature of the later picture.

Osborne Road (Seafront Road) c.1920. The shops are still in evidence today though selling a different range of merchandise. The premises of Twine the butcher for instance, now trades as 'Steptoe and Sons', dealing in antique and secondhand goods!

In the years following the closure of the Hayling railway system, the abandoned station yard, platform and goods shed were to become a magnet for local destruction both by authority and vandal alike. Happily the goods' shed was saved in time to become a small neighbourhood theatre, home to the Hayling Island Amateur Dramatic Society. South Hayling Station is pictured a short while after its closure.

Eastoke Stores on the corner of Rails Lane and Southwood Road viewed in 1930. The business still dominates this prime site which is now the centre of the holiday trade at the eastern end of the seafront. The shop trades today principally as an off licence and is just one of many stores and amusement centres catered for at this busy junction.

A social event eagerly looked forward to was Hayling's annual sports' day. It is particularly sad to think that even the very youngest of spectators witnessing the event in 1912 have, in all probability, passed on.

Girl pupils at Hayling Primary School display the ubiquitous slate bearing the legend 'Standard V1'. The year is not known although the style of dress would suggest perhaps c. 1912.

In October 1911, Howard Pixton a pilot with the Bristol & Colonial Aircraft Company, (his salary was £250 per year) undertook a series of over-water flights with a 'Box kite' aircraft using Hayling Island as a base and taking with him as a passenger, Lieut. Charles Denniston Burney R.N., who wished to investigate the possibility of operating naval aircraft independent of shore bases. Taking off from Larkhill, the pair stopped for lunch at Durley near Eastleigh before arriving at Hayling at 5.00 pm!

Secured for the night, the aircraft is tethered in the lee of the bath house and café.

VICTORIA HALL, SOUTH HAYLING.

Coastguards' Entertainment,

EASTER MONDAY, MARCH 31st, 1902.

PROGRAMME.

PART I.

1.	MARCH	..	..	"Advance Guard."	..	..	BAND.
2.	SONG (Comic)	..	..	"Nice Quiet Day."	..	..	Mr. SILLICK.
3.	SONG (Sentimental)	..	"Waiting at the Ferry."	..	..	Mr. PALLETT.
4.	SONG (Comic)	..	..	"And then I understand."	..	Mr. PRAGNELL.
5.	VIOLIN SOLO	..	..	"Simple Aveu."	..	Mr. GILBERTSON.
6.	SONG (Comic)	..	..	"They're Coming on Again."	..	..	Mr. PEARSON.
7.	SONG (Sentimental)	..	"Dolly Gray."	..	..	Mr. SMITH.
8.	DUET	..	..	"Two Johnnies in Love."	Messrs. SUTTON & GARDNER.
9.	SONG (Comic)	..	"Not for the Boat Man Breathing."	Mr. BONIFACE.
10.	STUMP SPEECH	..	On "Light."	..	..	Mr. PALLETT.

INTERVAL.

PART II.

1.	DUET (Instrumental)	..	"El Capitan."	Messrs. JONES and GILBERTSON.
2.	SONG (Comic)	..	..	"Latest Improvements."	..	Mr. PRAGNELL.
3.	SONG (Sentimental)	..	Selected.	..	Mr. GILBERTSON.
4.	SONG (Comic)	..	..	"Do You Like Jam?"	..	..	Mr. PALLETT.
5.	LECTURE	..	..	On "Love."	..	..	Mr. SILLICK.
6.	CONCERTINA SOLO	..	"Star of Bethlehem."	..	..	Mr. JONES.
7.	DUET	"The Champion Beautiful Brothers."	Messrs. SUTTON and GARDNER.
8.	PIANOFORTE SOLO	..	..	..	..	Miss FLEMING.

To Conclude with a

SCREAMING, SIDE-SPLITTING SKETCH,

ENTITLED :

"GRAN'MUDDER'S GHOST"

AUNT CHLOE.	..	..	An Old Woman.	..	Mr. BONIFACE.
JIM	..	..	..	..	..	Mr. PALLETT.
SAM	..	..	Her Nephews.	..	Mr. PEARSON.
HARRY	..	..	..	..	..	Mr. SILLICK.

GOD SAVE THE KING.

PRICE—ONE PENNY. *Accompanist, Miss Freda Fleming*

Hayling Island –
A Postcard Miscellany

Postcard views were particularly popular in the early years of the last century. This group of scenes from the reigns of Edward VII and George V adorned cards sent as far afield as Glamorgan, Worcestershire and Southsea!

Southwood Road, Eastoke, Hayling Island.

The Common, Eastoke, Hayling Island.

Westfield Road, Hayling Island.

Stoke, Hayling Island.

Beach Road, Hayling Island.

Manor Road, Hayling Island.

Alexandra Place, Hayling Island.

Sea View Terrace, South Hayling.

North Hayling.

North Hayling.

Fry's Cottage, South Hayling.

The Creek, South Hayling.

Mengeham Road, South Hayling.

South Hayling.

Vicarage Road, South Hayling.

Winton House, South Hayling.

Elm Grove, South Hayling.

Elm Grove, South Hayling.

Park Road, South Hayling.

Manor Lane, South Hayling.

West Town, South Hayling.

West Town, Hayling Island.

West Town Corner, Hayling Island.

Newtown, Hayling Island.

Sinah Warren, Hayling Island.

Monlas Cottage, Hayling Island.

St Patrick's Open Air School, Hayling Island.

Royal Hotel Tennis Courts, Hayling Island.

Coast Guards and St Andrew's Home, Hayling Island.

Pond Head, South Hayling.

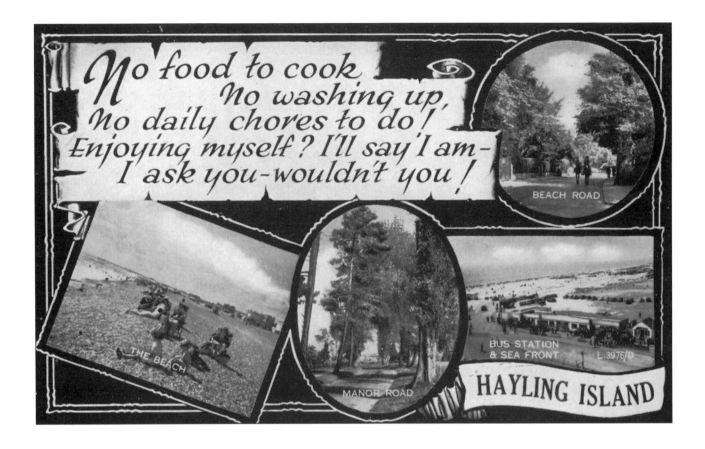

A selection of novelty postcards, bearing greetings from Hayling Island in the early twentieth century.

The Pycroft Family

Ancestors of the Hayling Island Pycroft family are seen at work in the closing years of the nineteenth century at a location in Milton, Portsmouth at a time when brickmaking was very much a local industry. A number of small family businesses operated in various parts of Portsea Island; a reason perhaps, in 1901, for the Pycroft's having migrated to Hayling where the competition was less intense?

In a modern, mechanised world, bricks are now manufactured in the hundreds of millions by processes which obviate the need to man-handle the basic ingredient, clay. In Noel Pycroft's Hayling Brickworks however, the raw material was placed into the 'Monarch', the cast-iron container pictured here, from where it was extruded into wooden moulds.

Mrs Valerie Pycroft worked equally as hard as the menfolk in her family and could regularly produce from her moulds up to five hundred bricks an hour.

Now removed from their wooden moulds, Noel Pycroft places up to 70,000 bricks in the drying 'hacks' as part of the curing process. Not a job for the faint -hearted or those with a weak back! After a lifetime in the industry he retired in 1989.

Alexander Mckee O.B.E. – Sub-aqua Explorer

Of the few resident personalities who have contributed to, and enriched the history of Hayling Island, none figures more prominently perhaps than the late Alexander McKee O.B.E. (1918-1992). Affectionately known as Mac or even 'Mad Mac' to his diving friends, he was a man of many parts and undeniable skills, his achievements affording him a place high among those twentieth century hero adventurers who have contributed so much to the history of Great Britain. From his early years (he learnt to fly at Portsmouth at the age of fifteen, obtaining his licence at seventeen years) he maintained a spirit of adventure throughout his life. One of our foremost naval and military historians, he wrote not only 23 books, but also magazine articles and radio plays each in the form of a factual documentary; he also worked for four years with the British Forces Network in Germany, writing, interviewing, producing and broadcasting.

Hayling Bay Sunday 18 June 1961. Fired with a passion for seabed exploration, McKee and members of the Southsea Branch of the British Sub-Aqua Club conducted an exploratory dive on Church Rocks, the site of the legendary lost church of South Hayling. The success of the day's exploration was crowned with the recovery from the seabed of the stone slab pictured here with divers John Powell and John Towse. This, the first of many subsequent dives, revealed a confusion of masonry on the sandy bottom of the bay, masonry showing signs of having been shaped and fashioned, sections of an ancient, possibly mediaeval building. Several examples were brought to the surface whilst others, too large and heavy to raise, including an eight foot stone column, were recorded and sketched in situ.

Of the several examples recovered from the seabed this distinctly carved stone has very obviously been hand crafted.

The activities of Alexander McKee and his diving friends took them to many locations on the south coast of Britain. This photograph, however, was taken on the occasion of the Solent Open Spear Fishing Championship in Langstone Harbour, 23 July 1961. The wreckage visible at low water on Sword Sands is of the *Irishman*, a tug belonging to Messrs Fraser and White of Portsmouth. The facts are: in the spring of 1941, the *Irishman* was towing the crane barge *Percy* when the explosion of a magnetic mine destroyed both vessels with the loss of five lives. (In the previous month, the dredger *Fravis* was similarly destroyed off the Winner Bank at the entrance to Langstone Harbour). Members of the Southsea team choose to spear fish among the wreckage of the two stricken vessels. The depth of water here at low tide is between 12 and 15 feet.

The Fraser and White tug *Irishman*, is pictured at her berth in Portsmouth's Camber Docks in peaceful times prior to the Second World War.

GREAT NAVAL SISTERS AT SOUTHWICK.

50
PHOTO RIPLEY
SOUTHWICK

Early in 1918, the nation commissioned Mr G. Menzies to design a series of eight defensive towers to be placed at intervals across the English Channel and so restrict the passage of enemy shipping; U boats, in particular,offering the greatest threat. They were to be manned, armed and have a system of nets strung between them. In the event, only two towers were completed at Southwick (Shoreham) in West Sussex. With the armistice declared in November of that year, the building programme was abandoned. One tower was demolished whilst the other was destined to replace the Nab lightship south of Hayling Island to where it was towed and positioned on the sea bed in September 1920.

The Nab when viewed from the shore of Hayling or Portsmouth without the aid of a telescope or binoculars, appears only as a distant feature on the horizon. In close up however it presents a surprising appearance! The boat pictured was often used as the ' dive ' boat of the exploratory team of intrepid underwater adventurers. Standing in the bows is boat owner Jack Millgate, friend and fellow diver of Alexander McKee.

The overcrowed upperworks of the Nab only add to its 'Heath Robinson' appearance!

In 1962, Alex and his diving friends instituted 'Project Solent Ships'; their aim to research and, hopefully re-discover, the Spithead wrecks of the *Boyne, Royal George, Impregnable, Edgar* and *Mary Rose*. On 19 July 1996, four years after the death of Alexander McKee, and four hundred and fifty one years to the day, of the sinking of the *Mary Rose*, a gathering together of one hundred family and friends attended St Mary's Churchyard in South Hayling for the dedication of this remarkable epitaph to his memory. The stone had been recovered from the depths of Hayling Bay by members of the Mary Rose Special Branch No 551. British Sub-Aqua Club, as a personal tribute to their friend and fellow diver.

The author believes it to be a particularly fitting conclusion to this brief selection of photographs 'borrowed' from the McKee family archives, to feature once again, the man himself, this time sporting the beard, which, in his later years, really did make him look like the 'The Old Man Of The Sea'.

Hayling Island in the Second World War

With the commencement of the Second World War and the 'call-up' of military and naval personnel, traditional barrack accommodation proved to be inadequate and less than satisfactory. The resulting overcrowding meant that facilities had to be sought elsewhere. Hayling, a pre-war holiday destination, now had a number of disused holiday camps lying idle, each offering purpose built accommodation for large numbers of conscripted servicemen. The photograph shows a squad of newly recruited naval trainees being instructed in parade ground drill at the former Northney Holiday Camp.

Personnel of the 57th Heavy Anti-Aircraft Regiment manned the defensive batteries at both North and South Hayling in the Second World War. The first of the photographs depicting life at the gunsites is of gunners racing to take up positions during an exercise at North Hayling.

Reproduced with permission of the *Portsmouth News*

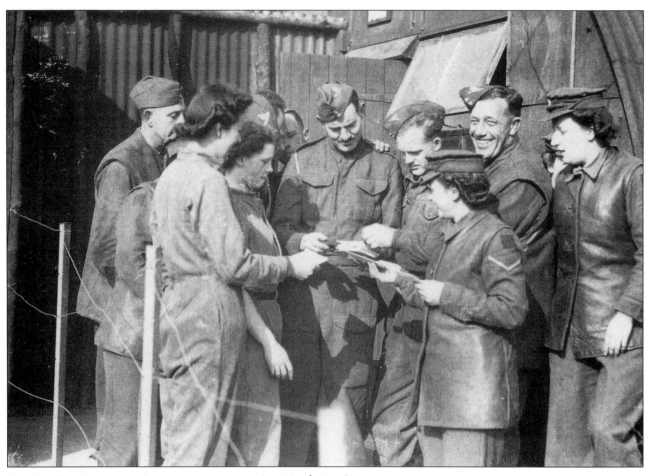

'Mail Call', always a welcome event, pictured at North Hayling.
Reproduced with permission of the *Portsmouth News*

'Stand down', time to relax, but never off-duty at the North Hayling site.
Reproduced with permission of the *Portsmouth News*

Call to action stations at the South Hayling site at Sinah. The guns are protected by the thick concrete walls; walls that offered but little defence when this site was bombed on the night of 17/18 April 1941.

Reproduced with permission of the *Portsmouth News*

The Sinah gun site has now been landscaped and preserved as a local amenity and memorial to those who lost their lives.

LEST WE FORGET

In memory of the men of 219 Battery
(57th. Heavy Anti-Aircraft Regiment)
who gave their lives here whilst defending
the people of Hayling Island and Portsmouth
against German air attack.
17th/18th April, 1941.

Gunners

James Bardoe	Reginald Knight
James Collingbine	James Powell
Arthur Farmer	Leonard Ward

(Royal Artillery)

The gun pit destroyed in the raid has been reinstated and developed as a feature of the site bearing, as it does, the plaque seen here which was unveiled and dedicated on Sunday 17 July 1994.

Several buildings still remain on the Sinah gun site; this example once had steel doors (probably long removed by an enterprising scrap metal dealer) and inner reinforced concrete blast walls.

This structure is thought to have once been a secure ammunition store or possibly an air raid shelter, so massive are its walls.

Dating from a time when an imminent invasion of our shores was feared, defensive Second World War 'pill boxes' such as seen here, were commonplace in our coastal regions. Examples can be still be found in many parts of the Island; this one is located at Sea View Road at its junction with Marine Walk.

Photograph by Glyndwr G. Jones

Because of its similarity in size and shape to Portsmouth, Hayling Island often played the role of decoy to deceive German bomber crews; diverting their attention away from strategic military and naval targets in Portsmouth. On these occasions, fires were lit in Hayling to simulate burning bomb damage and so draw the enemy away from the real target, Portsmouth. During these raids, Hayling suffered greatly, sustaining heavy bombing, much of it being delivered in the form of land mines. The illustration is of damage at West Town following such a raid.

Reproduced with permission of the *Portsmouth News*

Preparations for D.Day were carried out in comparative secrecy and included the construction of a number of craft such as this on the shores of Hayling Island. Stokes Bay and Portsmouth Dockyard also built units like, or similar to, the Hayling examples, as did many other south coast locations. No one could have guessed to what use these giant caissons would have been put. The thought that they could have floated and taken to sea was inconceivable, let alone that they would ultimately form part of a gigantic harbour on the French channel coast. The picture is of an almost completed 'Phoenix Unit'.

Photograph courtesy of The Imperial War Museum

Erecting the shuttering to support the concrete of the caisson. (The Ferry Boat Inn is in the background).

Photograph courtesy of The Imperial War Museum

The *Dredgewell*, in preparation for the launch of the caissons, is removing sand and shingle from the seabed to create sufficient depth of water to facilitate the launch. In the immediate foreground, are a number of anti-tank blocks, so placed to protect our shores from a sea-borne invading enemy. The far shore is that of the Eastney peninsula on the Portsmouth side of Langstone Harbour.

Photograph courtesy of The Imperial War Museum

Launched and fitted with armaments, these craft are assembled ready for the long tow to the Normandy beaches.

Photograph courtesy of The Imperial War Museum

On arrival at their destination, sinking the caissons smoothly and in their correct position was a tricky operation. Here a sapper is seen operating one of the many flooding valves. Note the size of the interior and the men in the distance.

Photograph courtesy of
The Imperial War Museum

There were mishaps when building and launching, the stresses being considerable. Here a fatal crack is forming on the caisson which ultimately was to be abandoned on a sandbank in Langstone Harbour.

Photograph courtesy of The Imperial War Museum

Destined to remain forever in the harbour entrance, a calamity was averted when the caisson was hurriedly refloated and towed to where it now lies on the Sinah sands. In the 1950s the *Portsmouth Evening News* reported the unit was to be split in two, each section to be a foundation for the towers of a proposed 'chair lift' planned to link Hayling with Eastney! In March 1960, the Mulberry unit was purchased by a London metal merchant with a view to removing all of its steel reinforcing; the terms of the tender requiring that no debris was to be left on the seabed. Almost forty years later, the situation remains one of… status quo. The photograph shows both ends of the unit to be slowly sinking into the harbour mud with the midships gaping at the sky.

With the end of the war and a return to normality, Hayling beaches were again made available to holiday makers and pleasure seekers. In the early 1950s, bathers on the west beach share the sands with the concrete plinths, upon which the Mulberry Harbour units were built and launched.

Recorded in September 1949, the following five aerial photographs reveal that holidaymakers were re-discovering the delights of Hayling's southern shores in the lean years following the Second World War.

The Kench, Ferry Road, Hayling Island, 1949.

Photograph courtesy of Havant Museum

Eastoke Corner, car park, Hayling Island, 1949.

Photograph courtesy of Havant Museum

Sea defences, Eastoke, Hayling Island, 1949.

Photograph courtesy of Havant Museum

Central Beachlands, bus station, Hayling Island, 1949.

Photograph courtesy of Havant Museum

Hut site, Beachlands, Chichester Avenue area, Hayling Island, 1949.

Photograph courtesy of Havant Museum

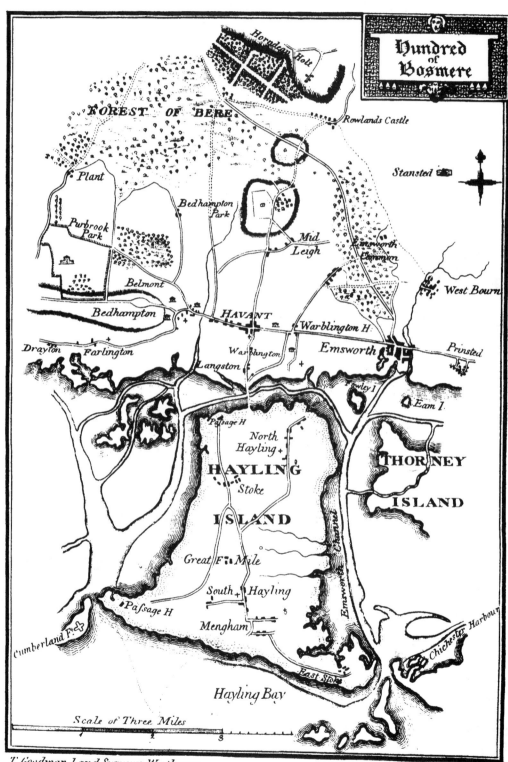

Ferry Point and The Norfolk Inn

In 1999, fifty-five years after the launch of the D.Day Leviathans, remains of the weed encrusted concrete plinths are still to be seen on west beach. Time and tide together, are achieving the destruction of the blocks, scouring the beach and depositing shingle where previously there had been sand. The Ferry Boat Inn, (the Norfolk Inn of 1944) is seen in each view.

The picture was recorded when the Ferry Boat Inn bore its original name, the Norfolk, the Dukes of Norfolk once being Lords of the Manor of South Hayling. The name change came about in the 1950s; a close proximity to the ferry coupled with a popular song of the time, 'Down at the Ferry Boat Inn', is the suggested and plausible reason for the change.

The earliest Norfolk Inn on the Island was the building pictured here. It is located perhaps half a mile distant and en-route to its successor at the ferry point. Having suffered several changes of identity eg. farmhouse, pub, brewery, and wartime base for the military, it is today a private residence.

John Marshall and Seacourt

John (Jack) and Blanche Marshall appear to have discovered Hayling in 1908, for it was in that year that he purchased a cottage as a seaside home for his infant daughter Joan who would be cared for by Nanny Walpole between parental visits. The later purchase of six acres of land enabled the building of a substantial and permanent family home, 'Seacourt'.

Large green-houses were constructed and a croquet lawn provided relaxation for the pleasure seeking members of the family and their friends.

Occupying an enviable position overlooking the Solent, the Marshall family, servants and friends gathered together here at Seacourt on 10 April 1912 to witness the *Titanic* sail past the Isle of Wight on her ill-fated maiden voyage. It was one of several occasions at which Blanche demonstrated her psychic powers and, feeling dizzy, clutched at her husband saying that 'the great ship would sink before it reached America'.

Daughter Joan, here aged about ten years, is pictured with her mother Blanche c.1917. While riding the tricycle, Joan, cornering too fast, toppled into the cucumber frames smashing the glass which she later admitted having buried to destroy the evidence!

At the age of sixteen, after suffering severe leg injuries, Joan impatiently abandoned golf lessons and, for two months, taught herself to play without 'going nearer to the links than a bed or sofa'. Incredibly, with her leg plaster removed only four days before the Hampshire County Championships, she went on to win each of the five major events. Joan's future however, lay not in her prowess in the golfing world but as the successful, best selling authoress, Joan Grant. It is from her autobiography *Time out of Mind*, that descriptions of her childhood at Seacourt are taken.

With so many visitors enjoying the hospitality at Seacourt and bedroom after bedroom being encroached upon, Blanche protested that, 'any further guests would probably have to "doss down" in the land-yacht sheds'. Land-yacht racing certainly did take place at Hayling and, whilst the sails indicate a craft of French design, the scene was recorded on Hayling sands, with Blanche at the wheel, in 1913.

A member of a wealthy family, John Marshall could seemingly indulge in and pursue his life-long interest in Real Tennis, building for himself at Seacourt, probably the first privately owned Real Tennis court in Britain. On what was an important day in his life this photograph records the occasion of the official opening of the court, 27 June 1911.

A player of international standing, John Marshall became the English Gold Rackets Champion in 1914.

Photographed on court in 1913 is Duncan Duncan Wilson the Seacourt Real Tennis Professional who remained in Marshall's employ until 1949. The twin names, Duncan Duncan were bestowed at his baptism because he had paternal and maternal uncles each with the same name and his parents wanted to be sure that neither would be offended!

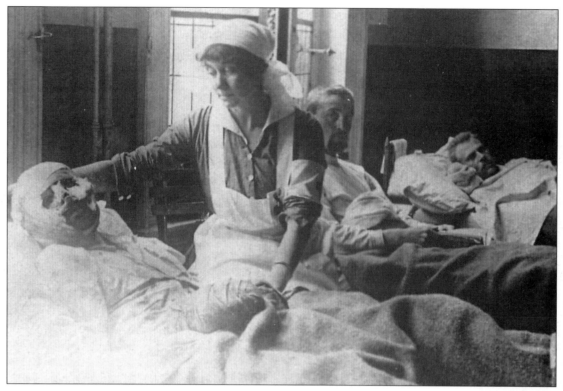

During the First World War, Seacourt accommodated a number of army officers attached to a musketry unit based on the Island; convalescent military personnel were also cared for and, later in the war, wounded soldiers were provided with nursing care. During the Second World War, the house was again brought into use as a convalescent home for officers of the Royal Navy, later becoming part of several properties on the Island known collectively as H.M.S. *Dragonfly*. Seacourt suffered bomb damage during the air raids of 1941.

Titled 'The Team' in 1972, this photograph shows the Seacourt Club board of directors, each of them active sportsmen on the Real Tennis court; they are, left to right, John Parker, Paul Danby, Ned Danby, Nick Danby, and Francis Snell. Unique among sports clubs, Seacourt merits an entry in the Guinness Book of Records as being the only establishment in the world where each of the five recognised rackets games are played, i.e. Tennis, Real Tennis, Badminton, Squash and Rackets. Other facilities include Fencing, Billiards, and Petanque. An added attraction is a modern fitness room boasting the latest apparatus where members can 'work out'. A fully licenced bar, restaurant and function suite complete the 'Seacourt' dream.

A MOSQUITO SUMMARY

by John F. Marshall, M.A., F.L.S., F.E.S.
*(Founder and Director of the British Mosquito Control Institute,
Hayling Island, Hants, England).*

I. HOW TO RECOGNISE A MOSQUITO.

A Mosquito is easily distinguished from other insects, notably (i) by the conspicuous beak or "*proboscis*" projecting forward from its head and (ii) by the *scales* upon the veins and margins of its wings.

The body of a MOSQUITO (which is a "dipterous," or "two-winged" insect) is composed of three parts: A. *THE HEAD*, which has two "compound" EYES and certain appendages described in the opposite column.

B. *THE THORAX*, to which are attached three pairs of LEGS, a pair of WINGS with scaled veins, and a pair of projections called HALTERES (vestigial hind wings).

C. *THE ABDOMEN*, which is composed of ten (eight only visible) segments. The ground coloration of the abdomen is usually some shade of brown or grey, frequently ornamented with white to yellowish bands.

The appendages of the head are a sheathed "bundle" of pointed instruments, known as the PROBOSCIS; a pair of MAXILLARY PALPS; & a pair of (15-segment) ANTENNAE. The palps and the antennae of female mosquitoes are *slender*; those of males, *bushy.*

The conspicuous parts of the LEG are the FEMUR, (linked to the thorax by 2 short segments, the Trochanter and the Coxa); the TIBIA; & the 5-segment TARSUS. The 5th tarsal segment is terminated by CLAWS.

The CERCI of female mosquitoes (and the FORCEPS, &c., of males) project at the extremity of the abdomen.

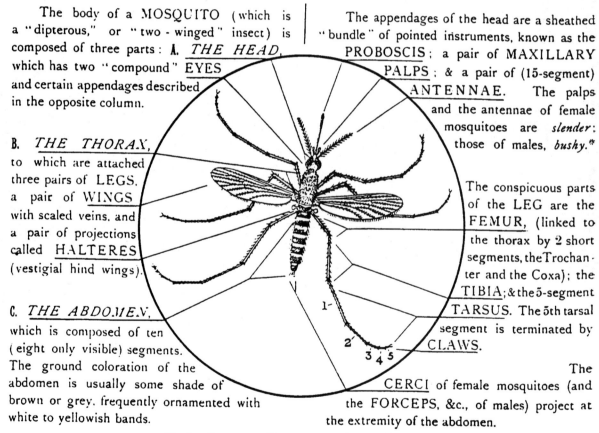

Fig. 1. PRINCIPAL PARTS OF AN ADULT MOSQUITO.

*The palps indicate not only the **sex** but also the **tribe** of a mosquito.

Hayling was, and to some extent still is, a breeding ground for the mosquito *Aedes Detritu*, 'the most far flung and voracious of all modern mosquitoes'. Jack Marshall personally suffered more than one biting raid from the creatures declaring, 'either the mosquitoes leave the Island or I do'.

Shakespeare wrote that, 'Love is only one of many passions'; a statement that could be applied with certainty to Jack Marshall for, while demonstrating his love for Blanche and his affinity for Real Tennis, he now became additionally devoted to the study of the mosquito. It could reasonably be argued that from here on, the mosquito became the third enduring passion to which he was committed for the remainder of his life.

An 11 roomed research centre was constructed here at Seacourt to house the 'Hayling Island Branch of the British Mosquito Control Institute' the founder of which was Jack Marshall. In 1936 in recognition of his contribution to the world-wide control of the mosquito, 'His Majesty the King was Graciously Pleased to Appoint John Frederick Marshall to the most Excellent Order of the British Empire'.

Encouraged by Jack Marshall, Mr H.J.Earney, the Hayling Primary School Headmaster, formed a 'Mosquito Control Class' where pupils, engaged upon field trips, would study at first hand, the breeding habits of the native mosquito.

During the 1930s, several private schools were established on Hayling Island. Illustrated is the Priory School for Girls. Boarders from the parent school (Lynton House School at Southsea) would spend holidays and weekends at this seaside retreat. A promotional advertisement reads: 'The school has three motor cars and is independant of public vehicles!' The turreted building can still be seen at the corner of Alexander and Victoria Avenues, just yards from the Seacourt Club.

Subscribers

John V. Abel, Langstone

Revd. Richard Acworth, Havant

George and Joy Adams, Hayling Island

Dave Adams, Hayling Island

Pearl Aitken, Hayling Island

Mrs Veronica Alden, The Olive Leaf, Hayling Island

Chris and Jane Alexander, Northney, Hayling Island

Mark Allen, Hayling Island

Greg and Doris Allen, Hayling Island

Sharon and Lauren Allen, Hayling Island

Ronald B. W. Allen

Peggy A. Anderson

Alma and George Andrews, Hayling

Doreen and George Andrews, Hayling Island

Richard D. Andrews, Havant

Mr George E. Arblaster

Keith and Shirley Ashley, Hayling Island

Alan P. Bailey, Hayling Island

Frank Baldwin, Hayling Island

Katie L. Balson, West Town

Ewa Barczykowska, Kwidzyn, Poland

Lucy E. Barnes, Hayling Island

Sue Barrett-Wren

Mr Colin Bayford, Hollow Lane, Hayling Island

Rupert A. Bennett, Hayling Island

Richard James Bettesworth, Hayling Island

Robert and Fiona Biggs, Stoke, Hayling Island

Ann and Bill Biggs, Southwood Road, Hayling Island

Rodney and Anne Bird, Hayling Island

R. Blackwell

Jean V. Blake, Hayling Island

Sydonie Bond, Westfield Glen, Hayling Island

Dilys and Melvin Bonner, Hayling Island

John D. Boulton

Steve Brades, Hayling Island

Patricia and Bob Brodie, Horndean

Christopher M. Brown

Hamilton G. Brown, Hayling Island

J. M. E. Browning, Hayling Island

Eddie Burton, Langstone (1967-2000)

Reginald W. Butler, Hayling Island

Mr and Mrs Michael Cairns-Todd

Patricia S. Card, Farnborough

Marian Carron, Dulwich

Mr and Mrs J. Cattemull, Hayling Island

Mr Kenneth E. Chandler, Hayling Island

Maura and Paul Chapman, West Town

Jeffrey D. Clark, Hayling Island

Gillian Clarke, Mengham

Pauline Clothier (nee Durrell), Hayling Island

Mrs Andree A. Cobb, Havant

Jeni M. Cockett, Brierfield, Lancs.

Michael E. Coker, Hayling Island

Stephanie H. Cole, Hayling Island

Dr Peter Cole, Langstone

June Cole, Mengham

Mrs Mary E. Coles, Hayling Island

Dr and Mrs J. M. Colley, Hayling Island

Christopher Philip Collins, Westbourne

Alethea Collins, Westbourne

Violet K. Conroy, Lyminge, Kent

Andrew M. Coombs, Selsmore

Leesa and John Cooper, Hayling Island

Sheila Cooper, Havant

J. E. M. Cottle, Hayling Island

Eileen G. Cottrell, Hayling Island

Nina L. Coutts, Langstone

James S. Cox, Hayling Island

Clint Craigie, Hayling Island

Kathryn E. Croft (nee Pycroft), Hayling Island

Sue Cummins (nee Durrell), Australia

Audrey M. Currie, Havant

Roger Dadd, Perth, Western Australia

Basil Dadd, Perth, Western Australia

Joyce R. Dallimore

Peter Dance, Hayling

Janet S. Davey, Hayling Island

Sheila Davidson, Guildford

K. Davies, Hayling

John Graham Davies, Hayling

Stephanie J. Davy, Hayling Island

The Dawe Family, Hayling Island

Peter L. Dawes, Hayling Island

Andrew E. Daws, Hayling Island

John and Rita Delahunty, Langstone

Jennifer A. Diment, Hayling Island

Joan and Dennis Doney, Hayling Island, Hampshire

Mr Eric W. J. Downing, Elm Grove, Hayling Island

Chris Driscoll, Hayling Island

Susan J. Duffy

D. J. E., Hayling Island. Year 2000

Val and John Easterling, Hayling Island

Mr R. P. C. Endersby, London

Wendy and Bob Evans, North Shore Road, Hayling Island

Myrtle Farquhar, Hayling Island

Jeffrey Fearon, Hayling Island

S. and F. Fisher, Hayling Island

Elizabeth M. Franklin, Hayling Island

Mark S. Freemantle, Hayling Island

The Full and Broadhurst Families

Louis and Heather Galea, Manor House

Bert Gannon, Hayling Island

H. Garnett, Hayling Island

Ian N. Garside, Hayling Island

Peter C. and Juliet L. George, Hayling Island

Kevin J. George, Portsmouth

John W. George, Cosham

Morag A. Gibson, Hayling Island

Patricia Gigg, Farlington

Raymond A. Giles, Hayling Island

D. J. Gillians, Hayling

Dr and Mrs F. H. Glanville, Hayling Island

E. L. Godsall, South Hayling

Phil J. Godwin, Hayling Island

Mr Roy Goldring

Roger Gough, Surrey

Mrs K. A. Gould, London

Jane Gould, Hayling Island

Clara and Frank Gravestock

Robert and Ann Griffiths, Langstone

Mrs Barbara R. Hall, Hayling Island

Edward S. Hancox, Oxford

Mrs Patricia Anne Harberd, Hayling Island

B. Harper, Hayling Island

Mike and Patricia Harris, Sinah Lane, Hayling Island

Mr Eric R. Harrison, Hayling Island

Eddie Hart, Hayling Island

Theresa M. Hartley, Hayling Island

K. Hartness, Blackwell, USA

Mr Nigel Harvey

Lorna Haycock, Devizes, Wiltshire

F. John Hayward, Slough

Basil Heather, Elm Grove, Hayling Island

Muriel W. Hedger, Northney

Tom and Jackie Henderson, Hayling Island

John Henly, Langstone

Alexandria C. Hick, Hayling Island

Margaret Higgins, Langstone

Stanley Hill, Hayling Island

Peter Hodges, Hythe

Dorothy and Sue Hollman

Betty J. Hollway (nee Russell)

Iris E. Homans, Sandy Point

Dr Trevor Hopkinson, Hayling Island

Mr V. G. Hoyle, Mengham

Cecily Hughes, Langstone

Felix Hull, Sinah Lane, Hayling Island

Miles Hutchings, Beauworth

Mr Michael J. Hutchins, Hayling

Shirley and Tony Hyman, Feltham

Peter G. Jaggers, Mengham Park

Mr and Mrs N. W. Jarmey, Havant, Hants

Paul E. Jennings, Hayling Island

Mr David M. Jensen

Dennis and Lorraine Johnson, Braco, Scotland

Symon and Ema Johnson, Hayling Island

Joan and Norman Johnson, West Town Hotel 1968-1977

Mr Glyndwr G. Jones, Bromley, Kent

The Jordans, Havant

Mrs Joan Jupe (nee Bradley), Hayling Island

Jean M. Killeby, South Hayling

Diana C. Kimber Lillington, Hayling Island

John E. Kinchen, Hayling Island

Andrew King, Hayling Island

Mr and Mrs J. D. King, Hayling Island

Stepehn G. Kirby, Hayling Island

Mrs Gillian Knight, Wade Court

Tracey M. Knight, Hayling Island

Mary Lane, Hayling Island

Krishna and Robin Langley, Hayling Island

Martin Lenaghan, Hayling Island

Richard Lingard, Liss

Lilian and Kenneth Little, Hayling Island

Graham and Deiredre Lloyd

Keith Lockyer, Hayling Island

Norman Long

Donald E. Loomes

Anthony M. Lunn, Farnham

Mrs Gladys Lyall, Hayling Island

John Macmillan, Havant

Mr David M. Maidens, Waterlooville

John Maslin, Sutton

Mr F. J. Masters, Havant

Mavis and Don, Fishery Creek

Gillian A. May, Havant

Joan E. McDonald, Hayling Island

Ed and Trish McEwan, Hayling Island

A. McIver, Hayling Island

Linda McLaskey, Hayling Island

Yvonne V. McRae, West Hayling

Jeannette Mearns (nee Durrell), Kent

Samantha J. Mill, Hayling Island

Tony and Hazel Mills, Sandy Point

David Millson, Hayling Island

Bryan R. Moore

John W. Morgan

Stephen P. Mowbray

Cecil Mumford, Hayling Island

Christine M. Murphy

Mr T. L. Nash, Sandy Point, Hayling

J. O'Shea, Hayling

Terry and Sylvia O'Shea, Hayling Island

Graham G. Oakley, Emsworth, Hants

Neil D. Oakley, Melksham, Wilts.

Philip C. Oakley, Great Kingshill, Bucks.

Malcolm A. Oakley, Sydney, NSW, Australia

Derek A. Oakley, MBE, Hayling Island, Hants.

Barbara M. Ogden, Hayling Island

Jessie M. Ollerenshaw, Selsmore

John S. Parker, Hayling Island

Philip R. Parker, Ex Hayling Island

George R. Parker, Hayling Island

Albert F. Parslow, Hayling Island

Shirley Paton, Hayling Island

Maureen D. Peacock

Mr R. J. Peall

Joyce Pearce, Elm Close Estate

Kathleen M. Pearson, Sinah Lane, Hayling Island

Beatrice Pellow, Hayling Island

Alan G. Perfett, Hayling Island

Mr and Mrs Norman J. Phelps, Hayling Island

Steve Pierce, Hayling Island

G. T. Pilcher, Southwood Road, Hayling Island

Mrs Joyce Pitfield, Hayling Island

John D. Pollard, West Hayling

Gaye Pope, Hayling Island

The Popham Family, Hayling Island

Charles E. Potts

Ron and Joyce Price, Bicester

Mrs Irene Read, West Town

R. A. Rees

Martin Rhodes, Hayling Island

Mark D. Richards, Selly Park, Birmingham

Betty Richards, Hayling Island

Nicholas P. Richards, Welwyn Garden City

Annie K. Richardson (nee Russell), Gosport

P. A. and J. M. Ripley, Hayling Island

Raymond E. Ripsher, Hayling Island

David George Roberts, Born 1933, Northney,
    Hayling Island

Margaret Roch, Langstone

William T. Rogers, West Lane, Hayling Island

Norman and Myrtle Rolton, Hayling Island

Revd Patrick H. Rolton, St Paul's Cray, Kent

David J. Rook, Eastoke

Norma M. Rowden, Hayling

Rosie Elizabeth Rowe, Hayling Island

Vera M. Royal, Hayling Island

Dr Damian D. Royal, London SW15

David Rubin, Hayling Island

Christopher F. Satchwell, Hayling Island

Melanie Saunders, Hayling Island

The Saunders Family, Hayling Island

A. F. E. Sawyer, Hayling Island

Paul Sayers and Ann Torode, Hayling Island

Ann and Brian Seal, Hayling Island

Linda Shaw, Hayling Island

Mrs Victoria J. Shortman, Elm Grove, Hayling Island

Victoria Sibley (nee Edmeades), Hayling Island

Stuart F. B. Simpson, Hayling Island

Eric B. Sivyer

Margaret Slater, Hayling Island

W. H. Smith, Northney

P. D. Smith, Ashtead, Surrey

J. P. C. Smith, Hayling Island

Don Smith, Hayling Island

Eileen Smith, Bedhampton, Hants.

Gillian Smith, Hill Head

Mr C. A. Smith, West Town

Mary M. Snarey, Hayling Island

Mrs Audrey Souter, The Witterings

Michael Souter, Southsea

Philip Souter, Waterlooville

Fred and Janet Southam, Hayling Island

Anna Sparkes, Sandy Point, Hayling Island

Tim Speller, Sandy Point

Sara E. Spraggs, West Town, Hayling Island

Steve and Jean Spry, Hayling Island

St Leonards Rest Home, Mengham

Betty F. Stapleton, Hayling Island

John R. Stephenson, Hayling Island. 2000

Mrs P. Stevens, Stoke

Mr Edward R. Stickley, Mengham

Pamela Stone, Sinah Lane, Hayling Island

Sheila A. Stoneman, Beachlands

P. M. J. Sullivan, Hayling Island

Terence W. Sullivan

Dr E. Sumners, Gainsville, Florida

Stuart Swain, Havant

Nigel Swan, Hayling Island

Elizabeth M. Symmonds, Hayling Island

Richard C. Symonds, Hayling Island

Mr and Mrs P. Targett, Hayling Island

Gerald G. Taylor, Eastoke

Mike Taylor, Hayling Island

Wally and Grace Taylor, Hayling Island

Jane M. Taylor, Hayling Island

Mrs Angela Teesdale

Paddy Thomas, Hayling Island

Henry and Jane Thurstan, Langstone

Alan Tingle, Hayling Island

Richard Tipper

Norman, Beryl and Anthony Tollow,
  Hayling Island

Ms Marie Towner, Hayling Island

Simon R. Trace, Tooting

Gladys Trigg, Hayling Island

Gerry Tucker, St Thomas Avenue

Ivor A. Turley, Hayling Island

Pat and Bernard Turrell, Mengham

Miss Barbara Rose Tye, Emsworth

Dennis T. Underwood

P. and B. Urand, Hayling Island

Mr Alan T. Vallis, Hayling Island

Mr Bernard Vaughan

Ken and Rae Vincent, Hayling Island

Tony and Carolyn Wager, Hayling Island

Linda Wakely, Hayling Island

John F. W. Walling, Newton Abbot, Devon

Nic Waterman, Amesbury, Massachusetts

Brenda Webb, Elmgrove

Dr and Mrs J. B. L. Webster, M.B. B Chir.

Joan Wells, Eastoke

Helen M. West, Hayling Island

Clifford J. Wheeler, Hayling Island

Desmond J. C. White, Hayling Island

Audrey M. White, Hayling Island

Ken and Pam White, Hayling Island

Ken and Anne White, Hayling Island

David B. Whitfield, West Town, Hayling Island

M. and J. Whittick, Oxon

Hazel G. Wigham, Langstone

Lynne Wilcock, Hayling Island

Donovan R. N. Williams

Arthur and Pamela Willitt, Langstone

Tony and Josette Willitt, Langstone

Derek Wilsher, Hayling Island

Eileen F. Windebank

Roger T. Winter, Hayling Island

Mr Robert P. Woolas, Havant

Roger M. and Dianne V. Woolgar, Cowplain

Edna Wright, Hayling Island

Peter Wright, Purbrook

Mr Cyril G. Wrixon, Hayling Island

Laurita H. Wrixon, Hayling Island

Clive Yeomans, Hayling Island

Grace Young, Hayling Island

John Young, The Kench, Hayling Island